SEEDS of WISDOM

Mike Murdock

VOLUME 1

ON DREAMS & GOALS

DREAMS & GOALS

DAY 1

YOU CAN CREATE ANY FUTURE YOU WANT.

- ❑ You will never leave *where you are*, until you decide where *you would rather be*.
- ❑ The day you make a decision about your life is the day your world will *change*.
- ❑ Move *decisively* toward the goals you have established.
- ❑ Intolerance of your *present* creates your *future*.

WISDOM FROM THE WORD

"Remember ye not the former things, neither consider the things of old. Behold, I will do a new thing; now it shall spring forth; shall ye not know it? I will even make a way in the wilderness, and rivers in the desert."
Isaiah 43:18-19

DREAMS & GOALS

DAY 2

CREATE A DAILY AGENDA.

- ❏ Your daily agenda is a written list of things you want to accomplish in the next 24 hours.

- ❏ On your written, daily "agenda"... decide your *priorities* in the order of their importance.

- ❏ You will never unlock your potential until your priorities become habitual.

- ❏ When you focus on your priorities, you will eliminate confusion.

WISDOM FROM THE WORD

*"Brethren, I count not myself to have apprehended: but this one thing I do, forgetting those things which are behind, and reaching forth unto those things which are before,
I press toward the mark for the prize of the high calling of God
in Christ Jesus."*
Philippians 3:13-14

DREAMS & GOALS

DAY 3

DOCUMENT YOUR GOALS.

- ❏ Take the time to write down carefully what you want to accomplish with your life.
- ❏ Writing down your goal makes you more decisive.
- ❏ The fifteen minutes you invest in making a daily schedule will be multiplied 100-fold before the end of the month.
- ❏ Visualizing your dreams and goals has power.
- ❏ Planners can predict their success.
- ❏ The secret of an achiever is his written daily schedule.

WISDOM FROM THE WORD

"And the LORD answered me, and said, Write the vision, and make it plain upon tables, that he may run that readeth it."
Habakkuk 2:2

DREAMS & GOALS

DAY 4

DON'T OVER-SCHEDULE YOURSELF TODAY.

- ❏ The wise refuse to consider too many goals.

- ❏ Only write down the number of things you know you will actually complete.

- ❏ When you over-schedule, your attention will focus on those things you failed to accomplish instead of the tasks that have been completed.

- ❏ Make time only for that which is worthwhile.

WISDOM FROM THE WORD

"Be still, and know that I am God: I will be exalted among the heathen, I will be exalted in the earth."
Psalms 46:10

DREAMS & GOALS

DAY 5

SET REASONABLE DEADLINES.

- ❏ Give yourself enough time to achieve your goal.
- ❏ Good things take effort and time.
- ❏ Be honest with yourself concerning your talent, time and resources.
- ❏ Focus on those tasks that you feel worthy of your total attention and time.

WISDOM FROM THE WORD

"To every thing there is a season, and a time to every purpose under the heaven:"
Ecclesiastes 3:1

DREAMS & GOALS

DAY 6

RESPECT YOUR DREAMS AND GOALS.

- ❑ What you respect, you will attract.
- ❑ Respect is needed for excitement.
- ❑ Excitement is needed for your energy.
- ❑ Energy is needed for completion of your dreams and goals.

WISDOM FROM THE WORD

"And also that every man should eat and drink, and enjoy the good of all his labour, it is the gift of God."
Ecclesiastes 3:13

DREAMS & GOALS

DAY 7

FOCUS! FOCUS! FOCUS!

- ❑ Focus on one task at a time.
- ❑ Abandon yourself totally to each hour.
- ❑ Remember that satan's greatest goal is "broken focus."
- ❑ Focus creates momentum.

WISDOM FROM THE WORD

"Only be thou strong and very courageous, that thou mayest observe to do according to all the law, which Moses my servant commanded thee: turn not from it to the right hand or to the left, that thou mayest prosper whithersoever thou goest."
Joshua 1:7

DREAMS & GOALS

DAY 8

TALK ABOUT YOUR EXCITEMENT.

- ❏ Enthusiasm breeds excitement.
- ❏ Your energy will attract others to your Dream.
- ❏ Thought and talk magnify anything.
- ❏ Enthusiasm is the only climate in which the Seeds of Success will grow.
- ❏ If you want to get others to get involved in your dreams and goals you must exude an aura of excitement.

WISDOM FROM THE WORD

"Death and life are in the power of the tongue: and they that love it shall eat the fruit thereof."
Proverbs 18:21

DREAMS & GOALS

DAY 9

MASTER THE ENEMY OF FATIGUE.

- ❏ Fatigue is the number one enemy of your progress and joy.
- ❏ When fatigue walks in, faith walks out.
- ❏ You can achieve more in one hour if you are rested than you can accomplish in eight hours if your body is weary and worn out.
- ❏ Rest your body - good health is life's first prize.

WISDOM FROM THE WORD

"And he said unto them, Come ye yourselves apart into a desert place, and rest a while: for there were many coming and going, and they had no leisure so much as to eat."
Mark 6:31

DREAMS & GOALS

DAY 10

DRESS APPROPRIATELY.

- ❏ Your clothing communicates an attitude toward the goals you are pursuing.
- ❏ People see what you are before they hear what you are. You are a walking message system to others.
- ❏ Even Joseph dressed to create acceptance in the palace of Pharaoh.

WISDOM FROM THE WORD

"Then Pharaoh sent and called Joseph, and they brought him hastily out of the dungeon: and he shaved himself, and changed his raiment, and came in unto Pharaoh."
Genesis 41:14

DREAMS & GOALS

DAY 11

TREASURE YOUR MENTOR.

- ❑ Your mentor is anyone who consistently teaches you what you want to know.
- ❑ It was a secret of Elijah and Elisha; Moses and Joshua; Paul and Timothy.
- ❑ Mentorship is accepting perfect knowledge from an imperfect man.
- ❑ Pursue and extract the knowledge of the mentors that God has made available to your life.
- ❑ You will never travel beyond your wisdom.

WISDOM FROM THE WORD

"A wise man will hear, and will increase learning; and a man of understanding shall attain unto wise counsels:"
Proverbs 1:5

DREAMS & GOALS

DAY 12

ASK OTHERS TO BE A PART OF YOUR GOAL.

- ❏ God never intended for you to succeed alone.
- ❏ What you lack is always housed in someone else.
- ❏ When you pray today, ask God to direct you to someone He has chosen to make a contribution to your life.

WISDOM FROM THE WORD

"Ask, and it shall be given you; seek and ye shall find; knock, and it shall be opened unto you:"
Matthew 7:7

DREAMS & GOALS

DAY 13

DISCOVER YOUR DREAM.

- Every dream is born or borrowed.
- It is born within your own heart or subconsciously borrowed from someone who has influenced you.
- Whatever creates joy and energy within you is probably an indication of what God wants you to pursue.
- Your dominant talent is the center of your expertise. Your success is *there*.

WISDOM FROM THE WORD

"And unto one he gave five talents, to another two, and to another one; to every man according to his several ability; and straightway took his journey."
Matthew 25:15

DREAMS & GOALS

DAY 14

PROTECT YOUR DREAM-SEED.

- ❏ God hangs photographs in your heart, of something you can become...do...or have.
- ❏ A Dream-Seed is the invisible photograph of a desired miracle, goal or dream.
- ❏ Abraham nurtured that inner picture of many generations of children through his promised son, Isaac.
- ❏ Guard, with all diligence, that Dream-Seed that God has planted in your heart, through prayer and discretion.

WISDOM FROM THE WORD

"Finally, brethren, whatsoever things are true, whatsoever things are honest, whatsoever things are just, whatsoever things are pure, whatsoever things are lovely, whatsoever things are of good report; if there be any virtue, and if there be any praise, think on these things." Philippians 4:8

DREAMS & GOALS

DAY 15

MAKE GOD YOUR DREAM-PARTNER.

- ❑ A God-inspired dream will always require the participation of God.
- ❑ One hour with God could easily reveal to you the fatal flaws in your most carefully laid plans.
- ❑ He who succeeds in prayer ...succeeds.
- ❑ Let God decide your daily agenda... and your dream will be achieved.

WISDOM FROM THE WORD

"Not that we are sufficient of ourselves to think any thing as of ourselves; but our sufficiency is of God;"
II Corinthians 3:5

DREAMS & GOALS

DAY 16

DON'T PURSUE YESTERDAY'S DREAM.

- ❑ What excites you in your youth may bore you when you are older.
- ❑ Be willing to relinquish previous goals that no longer stimulate you.
- ❑ Don't be a prisoner to your dreams of earlier years.
- ❑ You are not a loser just because you do not finish something you no longer desire.

WISDOM FROM THE WORD

"Remember ye not the former things, neither consider the things of old."
Isaiah 43:18

DREAMS & GOALS

DAY 17

FIGHT FOR YOUR DREAM.

- ❑ Don't let others distract you from God's assignment for your life.
- ❑ Avoid over-scheduling today to accommodate the expectations of others.
- ❑ Don't feel obligated to relationships that demotivate you.

WISDOM FROM THE WORD

"Blessed be the LORD my strength, which teacheth my hands to war, and my fingers to fight:"
Psalms 144:1

DREAMS & GOALS

DAY 18

CELEBRATE THOSE WHO LOVE YOUR GOALS.

- ❏ Recognize those God sends into your life to inspire and energize you.
- ❏ Acknowledge helpful insights gladly, and resist the temptation to become defensive and belligerent.
- ❏ Find ways to reward those who have made your goals and dreams come true.

WISDOM FROM THE WORD

"He that walketh with wise men shall be wise: but a companion of fools shall be destroyed."
Proverbs 13:20

DREAMS & GOALS

DAY 19

REFUSE TO QUIT.

- ❏ The secret of champions is their refusal to quit trying.
- ❏ Futility is merely a feeling ...conquer it and keep heading toward your goals.
- ❏ Create small successes when the large ones seem impossible.
- ❏ Even skyscrapers are built a brick at a time.

WISDOM FROM THE WORD

"For precept must be upon precept, precept upon precept; line upon line, line upon line; here a little, and there a little:"
Isaiah 28:10

DREAMS & GOALS

DAY 20

SOW A PART OF YOURSELF EVERY DAY.

- ❏ A Seed is anything you can do that benefits another person.
- ❏ Your respect for others is a Seed ...sow it.
- ❏ Your knowledge given to others is a Seed...sow it.
- ❏ What you make happen for others, God will make happen for you.

WISDOM FROM THE WORD

"Knowing that whatsoever good thing any man doeth, the same shall he receive of the Lord, whether he be bond or free."
Ephesians 6:8

DREAMS & GOALS

DAY 21

BE WILLING TO SOMETIMES DREAM ALONE.

- ❑ Every champion must be willing to believe in his own dream when others seem too busy or uncaring to encourage him.

- ❑ Every great inventor, such as Thomas Edison, faced waves of ridicule and scorn before their genius was recognized and appreciated.

- ❑ Don't forget to keep your focus on where you are going and refuse to be discouraged by the present circumstances that will soon pass.

WISDOM FROM THE WORD

"I will never leave thee, nor forsake thee."
Hebrews 13:5b

DREAMS & GOALS

DAY 22

RE-EVALUATE YOUR CURRENT GOALS.

- ❏ Never hesitate to reappraise your goals and what you really want to accomplish.
- ❏ Remember that your goals are birthed out of needs...and your needs are often seasonal.
- ❏ Celebrate every page of progress toward your goals.
- ❏ Don't keep pursuing a dream no longer capable of energizing you.

WISDOM FROM THE WORD

"For which of you, intending to build a tower, sitteth not down first, and counteth the cost, whether he have sufficient to finish it?"
Luke 14:28

DREAMS & GOALS

DAY 23

CHOOSE A PROVEN MENTOR.

- ❏ Those you admire, eternally effect your future.
- ❏ Choose a mentor who increases your faith in God.
- ❏ Learn from the scars of your mentor as well as his sermons.

WISDOM FROM THE WORD

"And we beseech you, brethren, to know them which labour among you, and are over you in the Lord, and admonish you;
And to esteem them very highly in love for their work's sake..."
I Thessalonians 5:12-13

DREAMS & GOALS

DAY 24

DEFINE THE TRUE CONTRIBUTION OF EVERY FRIENDSHIP.

- ❑ Each person in your life is a current...taking you toward your goals or away from them.
- ❑ Do not expect a 3 X 5 friendship to grow your 16 X 20 dream.
- ❑ The worth of any friendship can be measured by its contribution to God's assignment to your life.
- ❑ He who does not increase you inevitably will decrease you.

WISDOM FROM THE WORD

"Be not deceived: evil communications corrupt good manners."
I Corinthians 15:33

DREAMS & GOALS

DAY 25

ACCEPT OPPOSITION AS PROOF OF YOUR PROGRESS.

- ❏ Warfare always surrounds the birth of a miracle.
- ❏ Nothing is ever as bad as it first appears.
- ❏ Battle is the opportunity to prove what you believe.
- ❏ Joseph proved that opposition is the wave that takes you from the pit to the palace.

WISDOM FROM THE WORD

"In God have I put my trust: I will not be afraid what man can do unto me."
Psalms 56:11

DREAMS & GOALS

DAY 26

EXPECT YOUR SEED OF PATIENCE TO PRODUCE A HARVEST.

- ❑ Every dreamer must tolerate seasons of waiting.
- ❑ Waiting is not wasted time.
- ❑ Moses proved that leaders are not trained in the palace, but in the desert.
- ❑ Each day of waiting is proof of your trust in God.

WISDOM FROM THE WORD

"The LORD is good unto them that wait for him, to the soul that seeketh him."
Lamentations 3:25

"But they that wait upon the LORD shall renew their strength; they shall mount up with wings as eagles; they shall run and not be weary; and they shall walk, and not faint."
Isaiah 40:31

DREAMS & GOALS

DAY 27

INSIST ON TODAY'S PRODUCTIVITY.

- ❏ An unproductive day is an unhappy day.
- ❏ You were created to be productive ...to accomplish...to multiply.
- ❏ Any progress toward your life dream today should be celebrated.
- ❏ Each hour is an "employee"...give it a specific assignment.

WISDOM FROM THE WORD

"And God blessed them, and God said unto them, Be fruitful, and multiply, and replenish the earth, and subdue it: and have dominion over the fish of the sea, and over the fowl of the air, and over every living thing that moveth upon the earth."
Genesis 1:28

DREAMS & GOALS

DAY 28

TAKE A TINY STEP TODAY TOWARD YOUR LIFETIME GOAL.

- ❏ Champions are those who are willing to move forward an inch at a time.
- ❏ Stay in movement today.
- ❏ Break down your goal into many small steps.
- ❏ Progress creates joy.

WISDOM FROM THE WORD

"For who hath despised the day of small things?"
Zechariah 4:10

DREAMS & GOALS

DAY 29

GET MOVING TOWARD GOD'S ASSIGNMENT FOR YOUR LIFE.

- ❏ You will never possess what you are unwilling to pursue.
- ❏ Race horses never win races while they are in stalls.
- ❏ God rewards reachers.
- ❏ Your enthusiasm will attract the right people in your life.

WISDOM FROM THE WORD

"The steps of a good man are ordered by the LORD: and he delighteth in his way."
Psalms 37:23

DREAMS & GOALS

DAY 30

GIVE EACH HOUR AN ASSIGNMENT.

- ❏ Your life is like a train on the Track of Success.
- ❏ Each day God gives you 24 golden box cars (hours) to load up.
- ❏ What you place in each box car, or hour, determines the speed and the distance your train will move toward your next city of accomplishment.
- ❏ Make your life count today.

WISDOM FROM THE WORD

"Redeeming the time, because the days are evil."
Ephesians 5:16

DREAMS & GOALS

DAY 31

CELEBRATE WISDOM TODAY.

- ❏ Wisdom is doing what God would do in your present circumstances.
- ❏ Wisdom comes from the Word of God.
- ❏ Solomon said that Wisdom is the Miracle Key that unlocked life's house of treasures.
- ❏ Wisdom requires effort, time, and persistence but is worth the cost.

WISDOM FROM THE WORD

*"Wisdom is the principal thing; therefore get wisdom: and with all thy getting get understanding.
Exalt her, and she shall promote thee: she shall bring thee to honour, when thou dost embrace her."*
Proverbs 4:7-8